My Two Moms

Julie Murray

Abdo Kids Junior
is an Imprint of Abdo Kids
abdobooks.com

Abdo

THIS IS MY FAMILY

Kids

abdobooks.com

Published by Abdo Kids, a division of ABDO, P.O. Box 398166, Minneapolis, Minnesota 55439.
Copyright © 2021 by Abdo Consulting Group, Inc. International copyrights reserved in all countries.
No part of this book may be reproduced in any form without written permission from the publisher.
Abdo Kids Junior™ is a trademark and logo of Abdo Kids.

Printed in the United States of America, North Mankato, Minnesota.

052020

092020

 THIS BOOK CONTAINS
RECYCLED MATERIALS

Photo Credits: iStock, Shutterstock

Production Contributors: Teddy Borth, Jennie Forsberg, Grace Hansen

Design Contributors: Candice Keimig, Pakou Moua, Dorothy Toth

Library of Congress Control Number: 2019955578

Publisher's Cataloging-in-Publication Data

Names: Murray, Julie, author.

Title: My two moms / by Julie Murray

Description: Minneapolis, Minnesota : Abdo Kids, 2021 | Series: This is my family | Includes online
     resources and index.

Identifiers: ISBN 9781098202262 (lib. bdg.) | ISBN 9781644943946 (pbk.) | ISBN 9781098203245 (ebook)
     | ISBN 9781098203733 (Read-to-Me ebook)

Subjects: LCSH: Families--Juvenile literature. | Same-sex parents--Juvenile literature. | Children of same-
     sex parents--Juvenile literature. | Parent and child--Juvenile literature. | Families--Social aspects—
     Juvenile literature.

Classification: DDC 306.85--dc23

Table of Contents

My Two Moms

Cassie has two moms. They all like to go to the park.

Emily eats a yummy dinner with her moms.

William hikes with his moms.

They find a path in the woods.

Nora and her moms watch a movie. They like comedies!

Caroline learns how to skate.

Her moms help her.

Hank and his moms go outside.

They fly a kite.

Adam sees the ocean with his moms. They have the best day!

One of Mabel's moms likes to bake. They make cookies.

Glen hugs his two moms.

They are a happy family!

21

More Two-Mom Families

Glossary

comedy
a film, play, story, or television show that is funny or happy.

path
a track made by the feet of people over time.

Index

Abdo Kids
ONLINE
FREE! ONLINE MULTIMEDIA RESOURCES

Visit **abdokids.com**
to access crafts, games,
videos, and more!

Use Abdo Kids code

TMK2262

or scan this QR code!